Blockchain Technology

Starting Guide to Bitcoin, Blockchain

Technology, Cryptocurrencies and ICOs

THEODOR MAXIMILIAN MITTLER

presentation of the information is without contract or any type of guarantee assurance.

The trademarks that are used are without any consent, and the publication of the trademark is without permission or backing by the trademark owner. All trademarks and brands within this book are for clarifying purposes only and are owned by the owners themselves, not affiliated with this document.

WHAT IS IN THE BOOK?

INTRODUCTION

What if someone told you that you do not need any kind of mediator to transfer your money anytime you want and anywhere you want? What if someone told you that a certain way would ensure you do not need a bank to be between you and your personal business deal

You would not need to have an agent, an organization to lead all the actions you want to make and to control the entire process. There would be no single entity controlling your money and your transfer but you. Sounds tempting? It sure does, especially if you are not very enthusiastic about going to the bank. Many people are not really happy about something (or someone) having a constant supervision over their business.

Have you ever heard about Blockchain or Bitcoin? Welcome to the future. Most people either know nothing about Blockchain or they know very little about it. That can change if you read this guide.

The word Bitcoin probably seems familiar to you already. It does not matter whether you had read the word 'Bitcoin' written in some article, newspaper, social media or you have heard it in a movie that you were watching last weekend. This word has crossed your path in some area of your life, at some point. In addition, it will probably continue during your lifetime.

You have heard about it recently and somehow it was in your head more and more as the time went by. This new technology is simply something you cannot stay away from. It is very tempting and refreshing.

You perhaps already know that Bitcoin is called digital gold. Owning a Bitcoin would mean that you posses a very valuable thing.

You might not know yet what it means or what it is for, but you most likely know that it has to do something with the money. You most likely have no clue how the internet works either, how your phone works or how does the coffee machine make that extra special cup of coffee you crave for every morning. But, what you do know is what product does it give out and how to use it properly. The same thing works for the Bitcoin. You do not need to know precisely what it does, but surely you will know what to do with it. If you are still inexperienced when it comes to cryptocurrencies, you will eventually put the puzzle together.

Bitcoin is a cryptocurrency and digital asset. A form of digital gold. A cryptocurrency is a digital resource which was made to be a medium for some sort of exchange. It uses cryptography to verify the transfer, as you can see in the title. What you should also know is that Bitcoin is decentralized. This means that it is not dependant on banks and no single party can have authority over it. It is also the first digital currency ever working without a central government.

Therefore, there are many concerns about misusing Bitcoins to buy illegal products. This may be one of the greatest problems that this new trend can face in the future. It is believed that in some matter it can significantly have a negative effect on spreading the illegal trade.

You might find all of this confusing but take it easy. You do not really need to know how exactly does it function, but this guide will certainly make some things perfectly clear for you. After reading this book, you will have a solid knowledge on how Blockchain works and why its considered so perspective. You will also be introduced to some ideas behind the ever growing number of cryptocurrencies around the globe and you will realize many advantages of the new age and everything great that comes with it. This new age technology can potentially make groundbreaking changes in the world, economically and socially.

The truth is that Blockchain completely eliminates the possibility of one party holding the data by storing the data. That is one of the best traits of this system. One person, a bank or any similar authority cannot control it. This raises many questions about capital and money deals.

The customers do not have an address with password like they do on the internet (email, social media etc). They are given a special key so they can enter the network. There is a public key, which is an address, comparing to internet mode, and a private key, which is used as a password.

The very important thing to have in mind is to protect your key. If you lose your key, the Bitcoin network will not allow you to access and then you cannot prove the ownership. Practically, the coins will be lost. The recommended thing to do is to print it and make a "paper wallet" that you can take practically anywhere, anytime. The backup plan is always a 'must' thing to do because of all the cases reported when people not only lost their Bitcoins, but also lost a fortune.

Some people are more paranoid than other, but when you think about it - have you ever been afraid that central authorities could misuse their great power and it could affect you too? A lot of people find this as a very concerning issue and find Blockchain as an ideal solution to that – all because Blockchain's essential goal is to avoid exactly that! The goal is that there is no one standing between you and what you want to do, for example, transfer your money. Any type of misuse, single administrator and corruption is trying to be avoided in the first place. If you do not trust the banks or other types of central authority, maybe you should consider using Blockchain.

There are a lot of satisfied clients all over the world that use Blockchain to transfer their money and store some of their data. Once you upload some of your data, it cannot be lost or destroyed. It is a great way to prevent things from missing and deleting. The more you think about it, the more secure does Blockchain seem. Some people state that they see it as a more comfortable and safer way to deal with money than it ever was with banks.

Read this guide to gain more information on how does this system work, why it is good for, why it is potentially better than some other systems, what are the disadvantages, etc. Good luck!

BLOCKCHAIN EXPLAINED

The Blockchain is a specifically designed mechanism invented back in 2008 by an unknown party. Its purpose was to make sure that services such as money transfers and other type of legislatives between two parties go directly from one party to another. In other words, there are no contacts in between the process, agents to go through or dealers to put up with.

The idea behind Blockchain is to decentralize the power given to banks and similar institutions. They rule the world by having the majority of the money in their "safe" hands. Every transaction goes directly through them and it has to be authorized by them.

This centralized approach for handling this kind of services also gives them a lot of leverage that can be used to harm their own costumers. Customers become slaves of the system that will in many cases deceive customers or mistreat them from the position they acquired over the decades.

Without the purpose of "pointing fingers" other entities should be mentioned with the same directive. Governments work in a similar manner with their fingers caught in every ones business making it impossible to conduct private and secure transactions and to use other services that should include only the parties that want to make that same transaction.

BLOCKCHAIN VS. WIKIPEDIA

In order to explain what Blockchain really represents in this section it will be compared to Wikipedia. This is a great example because the way Wikipedia is organized is completely opposite to the way Blockchain is organized.

For start, the Blockchain consists of an infinite number of databases. This does not mean they already somehow exist, it means that every party, customer, or user makes his own database whenever he uses it.

On the contrary it was a practice in the world to always have a unified single database that can be accessed from different places by just a number of people with authority. This concept is used almost in every part of our society, and that centralized approach is what gives the just a few the leverage and power. Now to give an example, Wikipedia is a centralized entity which represents some kind of common knowledge that is accessible to everyone around the world, but it only exists on its central server.

This server is well secured and only a unit with jurisdiction can alter the content globally, although Wikipedia can be altered by any user worldwide, locally, but all of the content has to be approved by the unit of jurisdiction to be published globally. This works great for Wikipedia to ensure integrity of the knowledge provided. But in the case of transactions, and money transfers, if it would be possible to make a private and secure transaction between two parties of interest, there would not be a need for authorities and their control over the process.

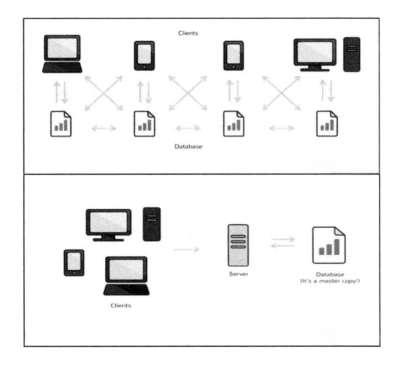

HOW IS IT MADE?

The Blockchain is built literally like a chain or perhaps a better example would be a train. Every car or a block is connected with his predecessor and his successor. Every block is connected in such manner so it knows where is its predecessor and how to communicate with him, as well as it knows where is his successor and how to communicate with it. This gives Blockchain a unique structure that makes it hard to alter data.

Every block, or to stay consistent to the analogy, every car makes a different database and it is created every time someone makes a new transaction. These linked carts make a whole train, or in our case a chain that makes it almost impossible to alter data because it will cause a disturbance in the chain and it will be detected. Data is also encrypted when it is stored in a block, or on a new server, or in a new database. Everything has to start from somewhere so there is obviously an origin car used to start the database. This process is very slow because of the number of transactions. More transactions mean more databases and more servers making the chain longer.

The conclusion is that Blockchain is slow and if you need a fast transaction, maybe this is not the solution for you. Nevertheless, if you need a secure and private transaction Blockchain will satisfy all your needs.

Its main purpose was, and remains to make sure the transactions go directly between two parties without anyone in the way taxing it. This takes the leverage from the legal firms and banks and other large corporations controlling the market with their centralized approach to this kind of services.

Blockchain represents the decentralization of the society and taking the power from the "big man" and placing it in the hands of the common folk. Even the origin block for Bitcoin, the first one ever made was made in the spirit of the decentralization, making it with a message disapproving the way the system functions at the moment. The construction of the chain is very flexible and a person with the right motives and the right knowledge of coding has no limitations when making the system.

DEMOCRACY IN BLOCKCHAIN

Referring to the analogy of individual cars connected making it the train, every car obviously has to be connected with something. Blocks in Blockchain work in the same manner. Every block is connected with its predecessor and successor as stated before, but the things that connected them all are of big importance in the system realization and they are called Nodes. These Nodes, apart from connecting the blocks work as voting poles as well. The system is designed so voting has to be done to decide if a new transaction can be made.

Every Node has to vote and when all of the votes are accumulated and accounted for the majority has to be achieved to enable the making of the new server, or to refer to it as a database, or simply a block. Majority of the votes of course, refer to 51% of the votes, statistically.

After the vote has been made and transaction authorized, in this decentralized system this means the people have voted, the block can be placed on the track. This track, also called the ledger represent a place, or area, that anyone can alter to its desire, but only the voted changes get through.

The ledger obviously records everything that is authorized by the vote. This is similar to the Wikipedia comparison only this time the authorization does not come from a centralized unit, but it comes from all the Nodes that participate in the ledger. As such the Blockchain is designed to be a decentralized system.

The node votes in this system make it slow. The regular centralized system would process any information or directive faster because it goes through only few authorizations without the need for a vote.

To make the Blockchain competitive in the real world, a solution had to be made. It was decided that to achieve better speeds of transactions Blockchain had to be made private. This makes private systems of several Nodes that number is prearranged and cannot be exceeded so the number of votes would not slow down the system. With this change a compromise was made between the speed of the transaction, as well as with the privacy and security of it.

In the security department, Blockchains like Bitcoin are trying to compete with the centralized existing systems claiming that their security, provided from several Nodes exceed the security level of the centralized system making Bitcoin a better option for transactions, in the terms of security as well as the speed concerning the private Blockchains.

CREATION OF BITCOIN

The invention of Blockchain led to the creation of Bitcoin. This creation became a very popular product that was soon used by millions around the world. Although such products already existed Bitcoin was the cryptocurrency that made a breakthrough in the world of digital cryptocurrencies.

Unlike a real currency, for example a dollar, Bitcoin cannot be accumulated infinitely. The creation (or: mining) of this product is limited maxing at 21 million Bitcoins. Digital cryptocurrency needs to be generated, like one has to mine it doing heavy calculations on servers, hardware or nowadays graphics cards (GPU's).

This product was well welcomed by people around the world with its ever growing concept of decentralization meaning it being limited only made it more valuable.

Bitcoin just as any product had a rough start with a small market value and this led to Bitcoin being neglected by its first owners making large amounts of the product to be lost in the process. The process of mining is an interesting concept that generates this valuable product. It refers to problem solving via personal computers instead of digging into the ground as the word would first imply.

MINING FOR BITCOIN

This is where Nodes start to be even more important. They not only connect every block, as well as they are used for the voting process, they are the ones whom generate the value of Bitcoin. This happens whenever a transaction is made. The Node used for the transaction gains some value in the form of Bitcoin. This is called mining.

In its early beginnings, Bitcoin was easily generated even using a desktop computer. For a whole year of "mining" one person with only one desktop computer was able to generate 200 Bitcoins. This amount today would be a huge fortune. It is almost impossible to generate even 1 Bitcoin with a desktop computer these days, the system has grown so much that one individual was just not enough to make any profit. This led to creation of different concepts and entities that are used to gain profit at the moment.

One of the concepts are groups of miners that work together to generate any income, this became lucrative and led to creation of larger groups that grew into companies that are able to generate even larger income which is distributed among the share holders.

The concept of Bitcoin was well accepted in China and their people overwhelmed the market very soon after Bitcoin broke through. Using personal computer systems, networks of Blockchains are generated to mine Bitcoin.

BITCOIN: THE NEW GOLD?

Bitcoin can be perceived as some kind of physical property although it only exists in code on the network. The obvious way to look at it is like digital money, with the right term of digital cryptocurrency.

The whole system exists on a network that consists of computers as the processors making it all possible.

These computers are all connected through the network and this way they are capable of detecting if a payment has been made somewhere in the world and recording the same payment on the already existing network. These transactions are never lost and that information is stored in the chain.

The blocks represent data stored which gets chained together and placed in the cumulative chain "The Bitcoin Blockchain". This place, where all the data stays, is usually called the "ledger" and this ledger is accessible to all who work with transactions or any part of the blocks within the chain.

Due to the popularity of the Bitcoin in the recent years, the ledger became a very busy and a crowded place making it a challenge when one wants to add new blocks to the ledger, meaning someone wants to make a record of a new transaction.

Another thing that rapidly changed over the years concerning the Bitcoin, apart from its popularity and network, is its price. This value definitely had its ups and downs, downs taking the time period of early days of the Bitcoin, and ups describing a mostly linear growth of the value ranging from cents to thousands of dollars to the point of a sudden drop in 2017.

This drop in the value was quite a shock and caused some disturbance in the stock holding circuits because it was a whole 30% drop of the complete value.

MYTHS ABOUT BITCOIN

There are several myths surrounding the term Bitcoin and they come from people who do not understand the concept of Bitcoin and its whole purpose. The most frequent one states that Bitcoin was supposed to be used as everyday money. People thought that they can acquire Bitcoin in the early beginnings and later use it instead of credit cards or cash.

This concept does look appealing but it is completely wrong. Why, you ask? It is true that Bitcoin became huge and the numbers connected to payments made from buying and selling Bitcoin are huge but the main idea behind Bitcoin was not it to be used as money. It was supposed to replace something material, something solid, something very old and valuable. Like Gold.

This material has been used for thousands of years to represent the value of wealth. Gold is the best reference to wealth one person can make today. Every other currency is measured in comparison to gold and it pretty much holds the market of value itself. Money itself would be useless if countries did not have gold reserves to back it up.

This is what Bitcoin tried to achieve, it wanted to be the one to be compared to, the reference of wealth and value. Its trading value is still not high enough to compare to value of the gold trading but some hope that a day will come when that will change and Bitcoin will rise on top taking his stockholders to completely new definitions of rich.

Another myth claims that Bitcoin is there to exclude the agents and dealers, the men between the transactions. This has proven to be not possible even with Bitcoin.

The code executed on the Nodes (=PC's) of the Bitcoin Blockchain is made by men who own those computers. And who controls the code also controls the way transactions are made. This obviously gives the owners some leverage over the users of the Blockchain.

This is not a problem if all the users would make different codes. But huge companies can change the whole market to suit their needs because they have large shares of the Bitcoin. The solution was to try and make new blockchains that would represent new digital cryptocurrencies and to try and make them without the flaws that Bitcoin has.

ALTERNATIVE CRYPTOCURRENCIES

The next thing you need to know to keep up the steep learning curve is that all the transactions are public when using Bitcoin and people should be aware of it! This is only in the case for transactions that were previously placed in the chain or ledger.

All users can access the ledger so it is public and that means everything in it is also public and accessible by anyone willing to read. Not all information about the transactions is kept in the blocks so only selective information such as amounts of money paid and the address to which the money was paid to.

Knowing that it is a crypto address and knowing when the transaction was done can be quite a lot of information to provide to random users. The identity behind the transaction is known only if the parties are involved with the service provider of the given transaction. Prestige universities have taken it upon themselves to solve this tiring problem and MIT has prevailed first. Certain professors from that university have given a solution to this problem and they managed to hide the information that was formerly public in Bitcoin.

The solution is called zCash and it is a different cryptocurrency used when people want extreme privacy when making their transactions. When using zCash your transaction is hidden in a very interesting way. Mathematical problems and formulas are used to crypt the information, so when you see the report it is like seeing a shake, you do not know what are the ingredients of the shake when you look at the final product, but you can trust that the shake was made exactly from the ingredients you asked for, and you can see that the complete quantity of the shake is consistent with your expectations.

One of the reasons Bitcoin is so revolutionary is because its concept, the idea behind it, believes in the power of the thought. If you believe something exists, then that exists for you, if everyone believes something exists then that exists for everyone. Meaning, if everyone would believe that Bitcoin was valuable, would it not be valuable?

That concept was used to create and expand Bitcoin, but although the most popular and generally known Bitcoin is just one of many blockchains in existence.

Another term that can be used when referring to blockchain creations is "crypto assets". One blockchain was created for the sole purpose of enabling people to exclude notaries and other intermediates when making contracts between each other.

This idea enabled developers to create contracts that can be considered smart. The blockchain that will be mentioned here is called Ethereum and it has proven itself in this field of utility blockchains.

The execution that supports this idea meant that contracts needed to be coded. Writing contracts in code enabled two different parties to conduct an agreement without any help from a system or a person of authority apart from the contract itself.

The contract does everything on its own making sure that only when activities from one party are concluded it expects and validates the activities of the other party making sure the contract is respected from both sides. The Bitcoin development is manipulated through the code made on the personal computers of millions of miners across the world. If they would join in with large mining groups they would be able, with joined efforts, to alter the origin code on which the Bitcoin Blockchain works.

This is exactly what nearly happened when a large amount of miners from China tried to alter the code by issuing an update on the network. This was a huge threat for Bitcoins identity and integrity and everything could have been lost if it was not for a great reaction from the Founders. The first members of Bitcoin managed to stop the update, and after this situation was handled there was a lot to discuss about.

The solution was made to present a substitute currency that can be used in a better more efficient and safe way. The product was called "Bitcoin Cash". Furthermore the prevention of such incidents inspired the creation of other substitutes in the terms of digital currency making Tezos in the process.

This cryptocurrency had great support in the community and was believed to be the solution to the upcoming problems encountered with Bitcoin, but instead of a solution, a problem was made, and it became a disappointment worth 232 million USD.

This enormous figure was the manifestation of the support the community had for Tezos. Everyone believed it could make a change. Instead of a change, status quo was accomplished leaving the project dead in its tracks. Great minds work together to provide a solution on the arising issue and they have decided that the change in the voting system would solve all the problems.

Following the idea behind blockchains in general, that the decentralization of the system would make it more democratic, creators of Tezos linked this digital cryptocurrency with a currency of its own, called Tezzies. These Tezzies, so called currency, are generated for the owners of the cryptocurrency, making them profit but doing it with a twist.

The Nodes created in this Blockchain work differently than the Bitcoin ones, and they actually decide how much your vote will matter in the terms of making changes on the code and issuing updates to the network.

This process is an ongoing one that is done by the machine on pre-determined terms and regulative. This way you cannot make big changes to the code that defines the cryptocurrency if you cannot back it up with the value of the same cryptocurrency, meaning big holders get big decisions and small holders get what is left.

ParagonCoin has raised over 170 million USD in order to open new and improved ParagonCoin centers. These centers have advanced technological electronic development and are fully equipped with the brand new trends in the world. They are available in all 20 US states where cannabis is authorized and therefore capable of accepting ParagonCoin as a paying manner. Multiple services are offered to provide the best value on ParagonCoin.

For example, a professional working area is provided. It is extremely important to have a place for business to take place. It is especially designed in order to gather all the important people in one place - including lawyers, scientists, doctors, reporters, mentors, professional staff and well informed individuals.

The ParagonCoin centers offer studios for professional shoots and interviews, projects and reports. Also, much time is invested in careful planning of events, organizing conferences and education on authorized, legal cannabis business. Paragon Coin members have special offers to join the ParagonCoin membership club.

The proof that the blockchain technology was a ground breaking discovery that in some way revolutionized how society may work in the future lies within the number of blockchain products being made around the world. All of the cryptocurrencies made have different ideas behind their coding, and different intentions of use.

The ones described so far, like Bitcoin and Tezos are made to both benefit the society but also provide profit, and where is profit there will always be a fight for power and wealth, and when the fights start the biggest impact is always taken by the society which those products were build to improve.

Apart from products with intentions to benefit each individual, there are some blockchains being made to benefit the society itself without potentially harming the individuals in the society. A great example of those is built to help secure the integrity and the future of the Internet of Things. This concept is rather new in the world and it is expected to grow rapidly until everything there is becomes consumed by it.

To help accomplish this, a new cryptocurrency was invented. And it comes from the land of great men and experts in this department, Germany. The name of the product is IOTA. Its job is to help machines on the network of Internet of Things. The main task, just as with Bitcoin and other Blockchains, is security. All the communication made between machines on the network of Internet of Things is supervised and authorized by the IOTA making sure the information stays protected at all times.

This cryptocurrency works with a little tweak in comparison to the ones you may have encountered before, such as Bitcoin and Tezos. It was not made to make profit, but it was made for the sole purpose of making the network work better. The Nodes on the blockchain within IOTA are not there to "charge" transactions because they are all accounted for by the block owners.

The benefits of IOTA, in comparison to other cryptocurrencies do not stop there, it also has a satisfying feedback time meaning the transaction, it does not matter how large it is, will be done in seriously short amounts of time.

The nature of the code behind this cryptocurrency is open-source meaning all parties who are interested in the code and its development can see it and participate in its future updates.

This makes it a system that can in theory grow infinitely. Every cryptocurrency made, at least the ones who have the support to grow and prosper, have their own Foundation which is usually named just like the cryptocurrency. In this case the Foundation's name is IOTA Foundation. This Foundation has made its HQ in Germany's capital, Berlin. Its primary task is to ensure that this product always comes with a free license.

Most of their work is involved with technologies they have investments for. Such project was made with Volkswagen and Innogy called CarPass, which was supposed to be developing Internet of Things around cars, and technology that can be applied to cars and traffic in general. The idea behind this is that cars can communicate between one another, having in mind that the future lies within autonomous vehicles.

This explains why projects and products like cryptocurrencies could be interesting for firms such as Volkswagen. Something that can provide safe communication between cars would be of great value in the future where concepts like self driving cars are not just science fiction. The implementation potential of this open-source project keeps growing and that became quite clear when collaboration between the IOTA Foundation and REFUNITE was made.

REFUNITE is known as the biggest missing people register in the world. The collaboration enabled the use of the IOTA platform to provide certain help with the ongoing wars in the world. In the war people get scattered around and huge migrations of the population happen.

This kind of system is what makes the line between the fiction and the reality blurry. A couple of decades ago it would be impossible to imagine having all your personal files and other important documents online and being able to access them without making the long trip to the official government buildings and waiting in never ending lines of people trying to accomplish the same thing. This open source product enabled such visions to come true and make the future one step closer to our doorway.

DIGITAL GOLD

Several Blockchain products in the form of cryptocurrencies have been mentioned so far but those are only the most popular ones. The number of cryptocurrencies in existence is skyrocketing and it has reached thousands in the world so far.

When these products are placed on the market they increase the general market value for this kind of products worldwide, and with such a high number of new cryptocurrencies the market is flourishing showing the demand is high for that "digital gold".

Some we explained so far are the most popular so in a few sentences lets recap on what we have learned about them. Bitcoin was the first one to encounter and its popularity is by far the biggest, and popularity like this definitely makes you have high expectations from the product. Bitcoin is now represented as gold, or we could say people want the community to perceive Bitcoin just as they perceive gold. It is something valuable everyone wants to have.

It is limited so not everyone can have it, and like history shows, if something is special and limited in supply it is valuable. The next encounter was IOTA, an open source giant that tends to make our lives much easier, this cryptocurrency will help IoT to spread all around the world making it functional and possible. A world in which kitchen appliances talk with each other to satisfy our needs, and cars know how to drive us on their own has never been closer to us and technologies like IOTA make it all happen.

After the Chinese tried to alter the Bitcoin code back in the days, the Bitcoin cash was created as an substitute solution to Bitcoin. It does not differ too much from Bitcoin apart from having smaller fees in comparison to Bitcoin in the start. The last of the giants is definitely a life changer and its contribution to the world's development has to be mentioned.

First personal phones became smart, then TV's became smart, the next step was other kitchen appliances and our cars and so on. But somewhere in there someone had an idea to make our contracts "smart". The platform that enabled this step is called Ethereum and the things this cryptocurrency does can only be described as beautiful. The smart contracts appliance is hard to imagine. As an example, I suggest we dig into the music industry a little..

The automation of the processes that a person would usually do during the fulfillment of a contract makes everything a lot smoother and faster. Hearing your favorite song on the radio? Well, if the singers' contract was made to be "smart" he is being paid for it at that moment. The copyright song comes with an attached contract that sends money to the author and everyone involved whenever it is aired, or whenever the agreement states.

THE REVOLUTION

The popularity of Bitcoin leads it to new heights every day with some users seeing it almost religiously, following any change and update. This kind of loyalty can definitely be admired and appreciated by the founders of the whole thing. Making Bitcoin into this revolutionary structure where its users become pioneers of the new decentralized system made this peer-to-peer Blockchain product popular worldwide.

Not many people do enough research on how this system actually works, which is to be expected because the final costumer should not have to know how exactly the product is designed behind the curtains. This lack of knowledge sometimes represents a difficulty, a problem to overcome in the general picture because the popularity this product made has made its value jump through the roof over the years.

When in possession of something that valuable people can get easily tempted to earn "fast" money by selling the coins to the highest bidder. This is understandable and everyone who has the opportunity to make it happen can. On the other side of the story, this concept of selling your Bitcoins is almost unacceptable in the world of hardcore Bitcoin fans, who have generated a whole subculture of sticking to their possession like their lives depend on it.

The term "HODL" is used to describe this behavior of not selling your coins ever. This concept has been noticed and taken in by other cryptocurrencies as well making it really hard for anyone new in the business to acquire new coins and join in the herd.

If someone has to blame or praise someone for this project years from now, he or she should use the name Satoshi Nakamoto because he and some of his companions are the inventors who made this giant. This means they are, although indirectly, to blame for making the concept of Blockchains public knowledge.

NEW PLATFORMS

So many things have happened over the past several years in the world of cryptocurrencies. These cryptocurrencies have created a whole history for themselves and now their progress through time can be divided into two revolutions. The first revolution was already mentioned and it obviously happened when the Blockchain technology became mainstream.

That caused the effect of rapid development and popularization. But, to acknowledge that some project has reached a point of high development in the history of its existence it needs to overlap on itself. For example, most of the world is familiar with Youtube. That platform had brought many revolutions, but for the cause of this analogy, only two points in time will be distinguished.

The point in time when Youtube became mainstream, causing the production of so called youtubers whose business involves posting different content on the platform and making followers along the way.

At the point when there were youtubers who were posting videos on how to make videos on Youtube it can be considered that the project did some kind of an inception and this is exactly the second revolution that cryptocurrencies are experiencing.

Instead of just flat out making new currencies with different features and gimmicks the next step to take is to make platforms which produce new cryptocurrencies, or they provide that possibility to anyone willing to have one or in need of a cryptocurrency. This was achieved with Ethereum which became extremely popular for the use of its "smart contracts". The platforms are to be made user friendly so they can go mainstream and be used to their fullest extent.

This platform provides endless market value solutions to the use of all kind of tokens, stocks or currencies. Some of the cryptocurrencies mentioned before were actually developed on Ethereum, such as ParagonCoin. There are some really big names standing behind this project in the business world, but definitely the one to mention would be Vitalik Buterin, who is one of the inventors and creators of this platform.

TOKENS

When having something so big such as Bitcoin in the business world just making havoc with its principals and in general making an impact on the existing society, many get the idea that they could have done better or that they deserve the fame Bitcoin holders are getting. This results in brand new codes with brand new people making them, with new brands rising up from the dirt and heading to the digital throne of cryptocurrencies.

In every business there are some people who are just too lazy to make the whole thing from scratch so they turn to copying, taking the original Bitcoin code and just branding it differently, or making a few tweaks so it would seem different. With either case the new cryptocurrency, or as we might refer to it from now, "coins" are not the one who started the mainstream.

This is the reason Bitcoin sits on the throne of the digital currency world making all other coins just altcoins (slang for alternative coin). They are just the substitutes, all those second places who may never be as big as the Bitcoin but they still might make a difference. Their impact is real and the market feels it as it grows bigger with miners all around the world mining for digital wealth on all kinds of platforms using all kinds of coins one day at a time.

Saying the altcoins are still worth our while and that they make an impact on the market is definitely the right thing considering the biggest altcoin out there is Ethereum, and as it was already stated before, this famous altcoin made the second revolution in the world of digital cryptocurrency. Others, whom are just copy paste creations of the original Bitcoin code like Litecoin do not share that particular popularity or the praise from the community they might be searching for.

The idea of making a platform for communication and all kinds of coin related topics proved to be dead on point because the Ethereum platform is just getting more applications with every coin raised.

The new trend is marketing. If you want your product to succeed you need to "get it out there", people need to see the magic happen in front of their eyes, and with this idea in your thoughts, it is now applicable to the Ethereum platform.

It is simple math and definitely something that the creators of the platform had seen coming and maybe even hoping for. A great number of young visionaries trying to start their careers are using Ethereum as a dashboard to place their ideas on.

The most important thing any idea or startup needs is funds. And the bigger the idea, the greater the amount of cash needed. So Ethereum is now being used to advertise ideas and other coins that are being made or that are in the process of making. Even other platforms are sometimes advertised on Ethereum.

The advertisement is used to bring the focus on the advertised product and gain support from the community in order to realize the product to the fullest. This is a painful process in real life and there are not many places one can go to advertise ideas and products in this kind of field so making a platform in such manner made it a lot easier and a lot more lucrative for everyone involved.

The conclusion of the Ethereum "inspection" could be that it is a multifunctional platform with a great impact on the market. Some use it to make tokens, some use it for coins, others for their own platforms in terms of advertisement but in the end it is obviously a growing platform that combines a lot of great aspects of this newly made market and it can be used as a studying ground to see what does the future hold for this branch of the business.

If it would come to naming some who claim the Ethereum as an advertisement window some might point out EOS. This represents a technology that is usually new and yet to be implemented, but the funds for it are still insufficient so people use Ethereum to gather some investments with the hopes of placing their coins on the market. In the coding world there are not many languages used to communicate.

This refers to communication in code, in the sense of making applications and blockchains and other familiar and popular structures. But, a couple of coding languages can be pointed out by far.

Ones like C++ and Java are the most popular and that gave the idea to create platforms that are consistent with the languages used, because different people prefer different coding languages and this way they can be in their "safe place" when making new applications.

COINS VS. TOKENS

Apart from coins being created on these platforms and in general, there are tokens as well. Tokens are a bit different then coins, but only in the terminology aspect. These are created so they do not need their own platform they would reference to but they use some that already exist. That is the situation with the Ethereum, that has multiple tokens created to exist by its original code.

This is with the applications implemented on the Ethereum and the trends maintained on this platform. Ethereum actually owns a coin as well, it was not designed just to be a platform for other coins, tokens, and platforms but it has its own cryptocurrency.

All of this was accomplished on the shoulders of the success made by the "smart contracts" project first made by Ethereum.

RIPPLE

Although it is hard to see, even the founders of Ripple are part of a revolution, as the freedom fighters claimed to be. Back when the project started it was maybe the case, but now with the ever-growing system of "democratic" transactions it is hard to say if you are running the revolution for equality and against corruption, when you are sitting on the shoulders of a multibillion giant.

I'm not to say if they stayed true to their cause or not. I could mention some men who were never a part of that cause instead. Some people place their trust with the government and other legal institutions finding them crucial for a stable society and with that thought in mind, they decided to be on the opposing side of this fight against centralization that structures like Bitcoin started.

Everything that has been done by blockchain structures so far was to decentralize the system as much as possible and shift the center of power on the other side. But this was done with privatization and complete disregard of the existing system. That may not be the best-case scenario when trying to see a couple of years in the future because these kinds of projects are a revolt to the already existing giants and that kind of shift in power may cause an unbalanced system.

A better solution may have been trying to update or evolve the already existing system with the concept of cryptocurrencies and other blockchain products. They will integrate into the existing system either way, over the years, but instead of hostile subcultures and similar concepts everyone could have been working together on a solution. The concept of Blockchain provides a unique solution to the existing problem of corruption in the general society.

With the development of these structures automation could be the solution of everything. Without the human factor involved there should be no opening for manipulations and other type of savage injustices created by humans on the wrong side of the law.

Without the knowledge of their motives it is impossible to deduce if these people were making the long game or just going against the flow and the society, but they made their decisions to produce these structures like Bitcoin and other Blockchains for government purposes and the need of other similar institutions.

They work with banks. One could say that they are enemy number one in the revolution. This type of market has produced one of the biggest cryptocurrencies in the world that is almost as big as Bitcoin with around 45 billion USD of market value in the year of 2017. This cryptocurrency has been named Ripple.

WHAT DO OUR BOSSES THINK?

Leaving the future aside for the moment, there is a more urgent topic. How will the Blockchain technologies affect the current system and existing society, and is the system ready for these upcoming changes? While some people are making new firms, getting jobs and generating wealth and income working on Blockchain technologies, the same technologies that make them all happy are endangering the lives of millions of people.

This is a pressing matter because the revolution in this industry is making the world change rapidly and new generations may be able to keep up, but what about people who cannot keep up with the change? Are they supposed to be left in the dust? Blockchain technologies are rivaling all kinds of industries and these are big industries with millions of employees whose jobs could be jeopardized if this technology gets the grip on the market.

The time to adapt is crucial, and there is just a little of it left. Many people do not know it is coming, many do not know what it is, but when the future becomes the part of their lives it is hard to say if they will truly be ready for it. One cannot emphasize enough on the importance of further educating oneself, especially if change is desired.

Several interviews of certain executives of important big firms in the USA show that this technology has a long way to go in order to become a part of our regular lives globally.

This is because there are already existing closed up systems in place working with what they think is good and right, and changing the concepts on which these industries run is hard and almost impossible without damaging the existing structure. With the right implementation however, the endangering of jobs and the lives of other people can be minimised. Ultimately, big changes can be achieved if everyone played a part no matter how small.

CRITICISM AGAINST CRYPTO

The main part of criticism is directed to the huge amount of energy that is used in order to process transactions. As the application of Blockchain technology rises, more and more energy is used every single day. In 2017, it is recorded that about 15 million USD per day are practically wasted. In order to find a solution to this great issue, the plan is to switch protocols from so called PoW protocol (proof-of-work) to the less energy requiring protocol called PoS (proof-of-stake).

This will definitely reduce the huge waste of energy that is lost and improve the whole process of transactions. If this matter was solved, many experts think that this would be the best money transfer there is. Low fees, fast and secure transfer that is available anytime you want it to be.

Some cryptocurrencies, like zCash, do not allow their customers to track the transactions. This is also one of the most valid issues that had been pointed out by the reviews.

Legal issues are very important to overcome because they significantly slow down any rising progress that was planned to be established. Many people are strongly against this because the main idea of Blockchain is to be transparent. Therefore, not being able to track transactions can have a negative effect on Blockchain. How did the crypto community respond?

In order to increase and gain more and more earned wealth, the crypto community wants to create their own authority. The central authority is self-regulating and it would be a huge step for the crypto community to make their own central government. Since the main policy suggests that there is no third party that controls the process, the crypto community has come up with the idea to make their own government.

BLOCKCHAIN'S 'HOME'

Thanks to good access to capital, good work ethics and unbreakable spirit, the United States represents the home to most crypto companies. Many cypto projects have been created in the United States and also financially supported. Another home to crypto projects is Switzerland. In Zug, a certain part of taxes can be regulated by Bitcoins.

The United States demanded that most ICOs have to be registered with SEC (Security and Exchange Commission).

In order to prevent US residents from claiming profits, most of the ICO's have put in restrictions. And one interesting fact: Although Singapore is actively involved in organising ICOs, Singaporeans are not legally allowed to invest in them. It is a great way to acquire and increase capital and seems to be very welcomed in the country.

In expectation of Russian regulations, Belorussia embraced its laws which certainly legalize ICOs and cryptocurrency. Belorussia is believed to be a solid ground to attract capital and foreign investments. It is believed that it can be a groundbreaking state when it comes to cryptocurrency by lowering taxes on crypto companies.

With the purpose of preventing deceptions, China and South Korea have prohibited ICOs until legal work is done and all regulatives are supported and solved. One of the first countries that vowed to become transparent and also to become the pioneer blockchain state is the United Arab Emirates. The country found it significant to stop the corruption and to be transparent.

By 2020, the emirates want all visa applications, bill payments and license renewals, which account for over 100 million documents each year, to be transacted digitally using blockchain. According to Smart Dubai, which is conducting government and private organization workshops to identify services that can be best enhanced by blockchain adoption, the strategy could save 25.1 million man hours or $1.5 billion per year for the emirates.

Some countries like Russia, South Korea and Israel have a great plan to make their own cryptocurrencies and introduce them to the world.

This project would have many advantages including lower costs.

'KEY' TO SUCCESS

How can you access the network? Like you have read, Blockchain does not require customer's address and following password, but offers keys. But, that is not the end. The given key must be kept on the safe place by the customer. Once lost can lead to great troubles. The best thing to do is to write it down on a piece of paper and put it on a safe place where nobody can find it and misuse it. An incredibly large percent of people, who do not trust the banks, ironically store their safe key in the bank.

Find the place where you can keep it dry and safe and most important – do not forget the place where you have left it.

Some people lost a great deal of values because they

have forgotten where their safe key was or because they have stored it on some electronic device that eventually broke and became unrepairable. Always have a backup to prevent possible nervous breakdowns.

EXAMPLE OF A BLOCKCHAIN COMPANY: CARDATA

It is very important to be informed about your personal vehicle. It is amazing to have a Blockchain company that will certainly take good care of it. The most important data about your own car is collected and put in the private Blockchain.

A customer stores his/her data via CarData Apps. The user advantage is always being up-to-date on car health, actual kilometers driven, service intervals and so on. Facebook for cars: Users can also compete and showcase their car. This app uses so called CDTs tokens. CDT is bought for example to prevent fraud in used car purchases, or to estimate safety of a specific car model for insurances. When you want to buy a used car, for example, you cannot be tricked if the car is signed up to the carData Blockchain. The data about the car cannot be erased or changed and there is no possibility that you can buy a car that is much older or has more kilometers on the clock than you think it does.

In order to create strategic and strong, reliable partnerships, carData's company (based in Frankfurt, Germany) connects with an open-source protocol IOTA foundation (which is also based in Germany, Berlin).

This technology will cover all cars on earth aim for the global market. IOTA technology already cooperates with many car companies based in Germany like Audi, Mercedes-Benz, Volkswagen, etc.

The carData project is already live and will launch its ICO in March 2018. More information can be found on their website at www.cardata.am.

INITIAL COIN OFFERINGS

Back to the Ethereum reference, it was said that this platform provides its clients with the ability of presenting or advertising their products and applications. It is time now to go further into the explanation of the possibility of fund raising on this platform. The number that can back up the claim that Ethereum is the number one platform in the world, at the moment, for fundraising is enormous. Billions of USD had been collected from all parts of the world coming from different types of investors, mostly private businesses.

Initial coin offerings, this is a term used to describe one of the platforms solution to the fund raising problem. It is in the best interest of Ethereum as a platform to have as many tokens as possible, that means developers have to be able to create new coins on this platform, and in order for their coin to succeed and be placed on the market substantial amounts of money are needed.

The idea behind raising funds in such a manner resides in what the developers can offer to attract investors. Unlike regular projects and start ups, where the only thing developer can offer are stocks of the new founding company, the cryptocurrency developers have the ability to offer anything they make valuable in their definition of the cryptocurrency, the only thing that is limiting them is their capability to invent and create a desirable product.

The abbreviation that is used for initial coin offerings is ICO. This application found on the

Ethereum platform is not the only solution to the problem called fund raising. Several other platforms offer the same deal, collect funds but pay taxes.

This is not always the most tempting solution because not everyone likes to share, or in other words not everyone likes to share that much. Kickstarter will probably work for your cause but at what cost is another discussion.

In the comparison with that, raising your funds using the free platform of Ethereum is more cost efficient if you have a way of collecting Ether to pay the procedure and use the platform. Ether would be the only limitation in that solution.

Another advantage that is provided to the costumer when using the Ethereum platform for a new project or startup is the ability to make "smart contracts". These smart contracts will automate the procedure of receiving funds and make it even more easy to acquire the money needed to create your own coin. For this application Ether will be needed as well because Ethereum does not function without them.

AUTOMATED CONTRACTS

Although much has already been said about Ethereum there are always some more details to be learned about anything. Now Ethereum will be taken under detailed discussion so everything there is to know about the platform can be inspected. Just to recap and in the spirit of being detailed some information may be repeated.

The basics about Ethereum, taken from the fact that it is Blockchain based, is that this is a project that supports the idea of the decentralization.

Another fact is that Ethereum used its blockchain structure to implement a system of automated contracts that have a way of ensuring that every agreement made in the contract is dealt without any outside manipulation whatsoever.

This means no usual suspicions of being tricked, the agreed terms will not be delayed, the contracts content will be available to the agreeing parties at all times and most important there is no unnecessary human factor involved. It is also well known that projects that come from the people, and work on the improvement of the society can be run on the budget of a non-profit organization.

The Ethereum is funded from the Foundation that carries the same name, making it the Ethereum Foundation. Just like the open source coded project called IOTA, Ethereum is from Europe, to be precise it is placed in Switzerland. ETH makes an abbreviation for Ether, the coin that is produced on the Ethereum platform. Ether is a very important part of the platform and any user of the platform must be aware of that. It is needed for all the transactions and any other kind of action made on the platform.

Unlike real money Ether is accepted by machines and they represent a payment method made by the users. Everything performed on the platform is connected through Ether. This platform is used as a place of application disposal. If a client whishes to buy an application from this Blockchain-based platform, he is needed to pay it with Ether, the only currency machines on this platform understand.

It is the same on the other side of the road because developers of those applications need to use Ether as well in order to put the application up for disposal, but that is the case only with applications that are based on the Ethereum platform code.

This kind of legislation made by the developers of the platform secures several positive results. The term "healthy network" would be used to describe one of those results, whenever the standard is high and the products are really first class.

Products on this platform are code oriented so they completely depend on the developers to their part of the job and make them first class. And of course the oldest feature on the platform, its famous smart contracts, can only be purchased or agreed upon, with Ether. This is of course only needed if the contracts are placed on the Ethereum Blockchain. Now let's talk about the stability of this platform.

In comparison with Bitcoin, which success solely depends on the amount of attention and love it gets from its users, Ethereum is more stable in the terms it has more to offer then just a promise of worth. It needs hardworking people with interest in cryptocurrencies that are willing to use Ethereum as the platform for their tokens and that is enough to make Ethereum run smoother than most of the cryptocurrencies in the system.

The myths that mistake some of the cryptocurrencies with real money are probably justified because of the current state of machines involved with cryptocurrency accessibility. Real money has its own ATM that people use to access the cash from their existing bank accounts. When some ordinary person that has not been involved with cryptocurrencies sees an ATM that can provide fiat money (known currencies like US$, €, etc. are called fiat money) via a debit card made for "crypto wallets" the confusion becomes obvious.

These debit cards can be used on all ATM's worldwide, both for cryptocurrency and regular currency but they will expectedly cost you more money. This crypto mania has produced thousands of ATM's around the world just to ensure the survival of the trend of the cryptocurrency.

If you have Bitcoins, there are a lot of things that you can actually buy with them. How amazing is that? It also sounds a bit strange and unfamiliar. Imagine that you can buy something with a virtual currency that you cannot hold in your hands, put it in your wallet, or even see it! It does sound a bit strange, but now it is actually possible to buy things with virtual money. It can be confusing in the beginning. Therefore, it turns out that you can actually go shopping or even buy a house by owning a certain number of Bitcoins. Check out the folks at Falc Immobilien in Frankfurt am Main, Germany for example if you are interested in buying a family home with Bitcoin. It's possible!

You cannot have Bitcoins held like pocket money, but did you actually know that ATMs for cryptocurrencies actually already exist?

There are also virtual cards and debit cards. Technology never stops to amaze with everyday inventions. You can literally go to an ATM and act like it is a regular ATM that you visit every other day. There are already about 2000 Bitcoin ATMs all around the world. Why don't you find out whether there is one in your city today?

POPULAR CRYPTO

How to earn gains from crypto investments? The best way to do so is to elevate the price of the crypto asset. These tend to get more and more valuable as more people purchase them. There are multiple factors that determine whether the price will rise or not. Those include economy, marketing, politics, etc. The investor is in charge of deciding whether the prices go up or down and will the assets rise or fall.

Like any other sale, there is a pre-sale when it comes to assets. For early inventors there is a great discount. The discount tends to get smaller as time passes by.

That means that investors which are early tend to get the best discounts, best prices and assets, therefore generally get the greatest ROI. Later, the discounts tend to decrease and, of course, the price gets higher.

First, there is a closed pre-sale, after that comes the open pre-sale and then the public sale. During the public sale the bonuses are removed in steps and in the end – exchange listings.

The best thing to do is to get the discounts as long as you can and get the best offers and the best prices for you.

WHITE PAPER

The skills of taking money from people come to the expression when it is time to make the "Whitepaper". This paper is needed when Initial coin offerings succeed and investors show up with the money searching for projects worth their money and their time. Teams of people are needed to figure out what to give in order to gain investments without giving away the whole company before it even started.

That is when the creativity of the developers of the cryptocurrencies comes to view. They need to make promises that investors will believe in, and to make them satisfied and feel like they actually made money, instead of give it away.

When the coin hits the market it is expected to have an increase in worth, this increase should happen over time and it should bring much interest to the investors because the most often promise they get when it comes to cryptocurrencies is that promise of coins.

They get them while they are cheap and if the project succeeds their worth can multiply in thousands of times giving the investors their money back, with interest. These promises are made between the development team and the investors and they are usually sealed with a smart contract that will make sure all the promises are kept. The "Whitepaper" mentioned before is the thing usually used in the opening discussion before the contract is sealed.

Some examples of these promises can look something like, the promise of percentage payment of monthly income to the owners of the coins, or in some cases of tokens.

CONCLUSION

Many experts in the world of economy, business and money, from all around the world, predict that Blockchain could change the way the world we know today functions. It is believed that it is a foundational system that could overcome all the existing models of economic systems. It not only has the potential to replace the existing systems, but also to represent the base of creating the new ones.

We are not yet at a point where systems are replaced, but you never know. It might happen sooner than faster. Even though we cannot be sure how much time will pass before it really has an enormous impact on the existing systems, you better be prepared for that day. Join a Forum or Group to discuss Cryptocurrencies or bring it up over a beer with friends, you will be surprised how many people like to talk about it or are already invested.

Blockchain is considered to be one of the best creations, a revolution in the field of technology and that it is 'that missing part' the internet needed. However, some other experts in the field are not very positive about this system claiming that many illegal actions can be done through this system including illegal trade.

One of the worst problems that occur in the world is corruption. Corruption overtakes many segments of human life and surely creates a lot of problems in the world of economics and business. People are not organized systems that are programmed and controlled on the very beginning of living.

Creating the revolution and implementing the same could be the solution to end money corruption. By avoiding central governments, banks and other mediators, it is believed that corruption could also be avoided.

Blockchain cannot be controlled by a third party and is transparent. By definition, it is a public system. It is almost impossible for someone to take over the whole network. Even if someone managed to do that, taking over the network in order to capture Bitcoins would literally have the worst possible effect – it would make Bitcoins lose their value. What would be the point then? Bitcoins would become completely useless by losing their value. Therefore, this system is described also as a very safe, secure system that will bring positive change in the world.

What happens on the Blockchain literally stays on the Blockchain. Once you do confirm your transaction, it cannot be changed and more important – no one can change it for you.

Nobody can manipulate your transactions or treat unfairly. This peer-to-peer relation can ensure safe relations between the sender and the recipient, wherever they are. When it comes to privacy, nobody can access the data that was sent but the recipient and, of course, the sender.

Usually, people are really annoyed by the fact that by the conventional banks' protocol, transactions take more time than people want to. Nobody likes to wait for anything, especially if it has to do with something about his or her personal possessions.

Sometimes it can last for days. Banks have their normal work time and that is surely not 24/7. Time zones can also slow down the process and delay the transactions. When it comes to Blockchain, the bare process is much faster. Everything that happens on the Blockchain is updated immediately and automatically.

No more waiting for days in order for money to transfer to another part of the planet. The process is very accurate and fast and one of the favorite customers' traits. No more waiting, impatience and nervous clients.

The Founder of Ethereum said: "Blockchain solves the problem of manipulation. When I speak about it in the West, people say they trust Google, Facebook, or their banks. But the rest of the world does not trust organizations and corporations that much — I mean Africa, India, the Eastern Europe, or Russia. It's not about the places where people are really rich. Blockchain's opportunities are the highest in the countries that have not reached that level yet."

Avoiding transaction fees is also one of the most tempting traits of Blockchain. Who would not want to avoid all the paper work, transaction fees, waiting in lines, extra money that has to be paid? Blockchain provides a great service that can avoid so many things that almost all people hate.

In addition, if you distribute your data you do not need to worry about your data being lost or stolen.

It is an amazing opportunity to protect intellectual properties. Copyright issues are very common nowadays. Many people have had problems connected to that matter and decided not to continue sharing their knowledge, thoughts and work. In order to prevent that, Blockchain offers smart contracts that have been mentioned in more detail earlier in the text.

It is an amazing opportunity to protect your rights and earn money at the same time. Smart contracts are your opportunity to protect what you create and to share it with the world without being afraid that someone will steal it or misuse it. This is just one of the great things that Blockchain offers.

Blockchain has enabled fast transfer, but also enabled a very cheap way to transfer too. The rise of Bitcoin brought fast and cheap money transactions and all kinds of benefits that were unimaginable before.

Other international payment methods have their flaws that Blockchain can cover. For example, other payment methods sometimes require high fees, have specific limitations like how much money you can transfer, where you can transfer it, length of transfer that we have talked about before and other disadvantages.

This is the reason why many business people tend to switch to cryptocurrencies. And not only business related people, but also regular people who simply want to send some money in short notice. Bitcoin provides more secure transactions, less restrictions and more opportunities. It is believed that at some point people will find standard transactions unnecessary and full of flaws.

It is on you to decide whether you think this is a great project that will help so many people in the world or it simply is not for you. Have a closer look at all advantages and disadvantages of Blockchain and decide what is right for you.

I hope this guide helped you understand at least the basics better, that you are now more familiar with certain terms around Blockchain and how the system works. You definitely know more than you have known before. It is not an easy thing to understand everything at once. Go out there and dig deeper. There is so much to be explored.